>YOU+DO-THE÷MATH

Practice your math and train with the best.

FLYA
JET FIGHTER

HILARY KOLL AND **STEVE MILLS**
ILLUSTRATED BY **VLADIMIR ALEKSIC**

QEB Publishing

Editor: Jon Richards
Designers: Ed Simkins and Jonathan Vipond
Illustrator: Vladmir Aleksic

QEB Editorial Director: Victoria Garrard
QEB Art Director: Laura Roberts-Jensen
QEB Editor: Tasha Percy
QEB Designer: Krina Patel

First published in the United States by
QEB Publishing, Inc.
3 Wrigley, Suite A
Irvine, CA 92618

www.qed-publishing.co.uk

A CIP record for this book is available from
the Library of Congress.

ISBN 978 1 60992 731 8

Printed in China

CONTENTS

Hi, my name is Katie and I'm a pilot. I'm here to show you how math can help you fly a jet fighter.

Words in **bold** are explained in the glossary on page 32.

HIGH SPEEDS

Jet fighters are fast, small, and very maneuverable. They are used in many different roles, including air-to-air combat.

You have been given command of a squadron of jet fighters and their pilots.

Jet fighters are powered by jet engines. These work by air being sucked into the engine, compressed (squashed into a smaller volume), mixed with fuel, and then burned.

Air sucked in

Blast of hot gases

Burning fuel creates a powerful blast of hot gases, which rush out of the back of the engine, pushing the aircraft forward.

Most jet fighters go faster than the speed of sound—which is about 760 miles per hour (mph) at sea level. Speeds faster than sound are known as supersonic speeds.

The speed of sound gets slower as the jet fighters climb higher up into the atmosphere.

1 How much faster than the speed of sound is a jet fighter going when it is at:

a) 820 mph? b) 950 mph?
c) 990 mph? d) 1,010 mph?
e) 1,300 mph? f) 1,560 mph?

2 If a jet fighter is flying at the speed of sound this is known as Mach 1 (pronounced 'Mock one'). If it is flying twice the speed of sound, this is known as Mach 2. What speed is Mach 2?

3 If a car is driving at 19 mph, how many times faster than 19 mph is:
a) Mach 1?
b) Mach 2?

4 Work out these speeds:

a) Mach 1·1 is 75 mph faster than Mach 1. What speed is Mach 1·1?
b) Mach 1·2 is 150 mph faster than Mach 1. What speed is Mach 1·2?
c) Mach 1·9 is 75 mph slower than Mach 2. What speed is Mach 1·9?
d) Mach 1·5 is halfway between Mach 1 and Mach 2. What speed is Mach 1·5?

WHAT ABOUT THIS?
Find out the speeds of some other vehicles and see how they compare to a supersonic jet fighter.

DIFFERENT TYPES OF JET FIGHTER

The jet fighter you will fly is called the F-22 Raptor.
The letter "F" in its name stands for "fighter."

During your flight missions, you might come up against fighters from other air forces. Look at the data in this table to compare some of these jet fighters to your own.

JET FIGHTER TYPES

	F-22 RAPTOR	EUROFIGHTER TYPHOON	F-35 LIGHTNING II	CHENGDU J-10
Crew	1	1	1	1
Length	62.1 ft	52.4 ft	51.4 ft	50.8 ft
Wingspan	44.5 ft	35.9 ft	35 ft	31.9 ft
Height	16.66 ft	17.3 ft	14.2 ft	17.81 ft
Wing **area**	840 ft²	551 ft²	640 ft²	356 ft²
Max. takeoff weight	83,500 lb	51,800 lb	70,000 lb	42,500 lb
Max. speed at high altitude	Mach 2.25	Mach 2	Mach 1.6	Mach 2.2

THE HISTORY OF JET FIGHTERS

Part of your training involves learning about the history of jet fighters and their use in combat.

This **timeline** shows some of the key events in the history of jet fighters.

The turbojet was invented by Frank Whittle.

The Italian Caproni Campini N.1 motorjet prototype was launched.

Britain's Gloster Meteor entered service and was used to defend London against Germany's V-1 missile (known as the "doodlebug").

1930 1939 1940 1942 1944

The German Messerschmitt Me 262 became the first jet used in combat.

The first turbojet aircraft to fly was the German Heinkel He 178.

1 What happened 24 years before the year 1954?

2 Which fighter entered service 16 years after 1939?

3 How many years after the first flight of the Heinkel He 178 did the MiG-19 enter service?

4 How many years after the first turbojet aircraft were launched did the Eurofighter Typhoon enter service?

5 Which fighter entered service 51 years after the Hawker Hunter?

6 How long before the maiden flight of the Chengdu J-20 did the Gloster Meteor enter service?

The Chinese Chengdu J-20 made its first flight.

The British single-seat jet fighter, the Hawker Hunter, entered service.

The Eurofighter Typhoon entered service.

1950   1954 1955   2003 2005 2011

The first jet-to-jet dogfight in history occurred over Korea.

The Russian MiG-19 entered service.

The F-22 Raptor entered service.

WHAT ABOUT THIS?
Choose four events from the timeline and work out how many years ago they happened.

JET FIGHTER USES

Every mission you fly will be different! One day you could be involved in air-to-air combat and the next you could be carrying out a vital role escorting other aircraft.

Depending on the mission, a jet fighter could be used for tasks such as reconnaissance (finding out what the enemy is doing)...

...attacking targets on the ground...

...air support for ground troops...

...or escorting other aircraft.

This pie chart shows the proportion of hours that one jet fighter spends doing different operations.

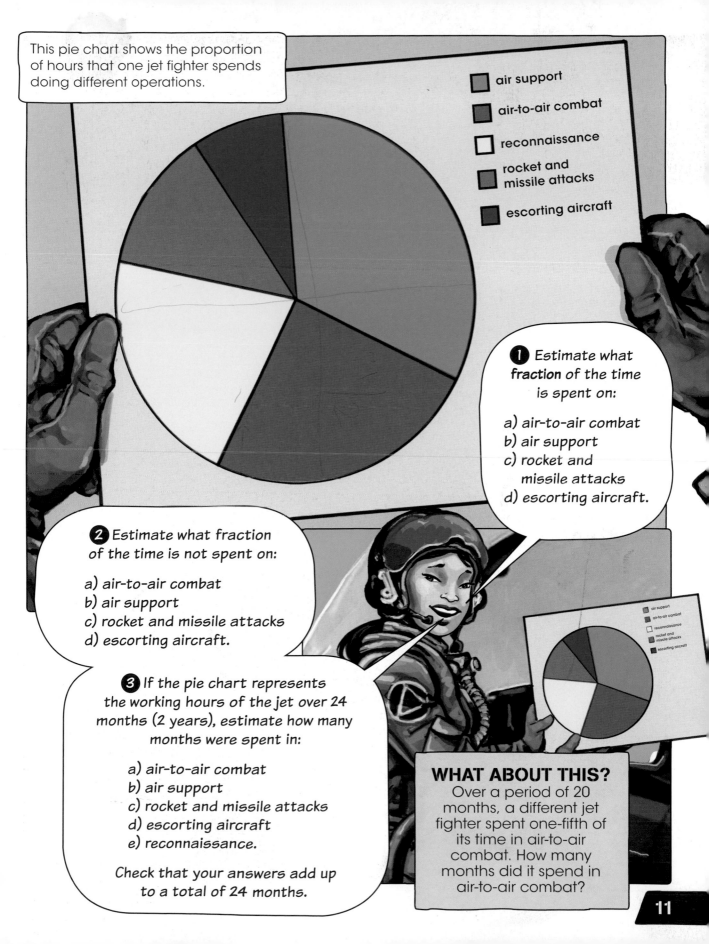

air support

air-to-air combat

reconnaissance

rocket and missile attacks

escorting aircraft

1 Estimate what **fraction** of the time is spent on:

a) air-to-air combat
b) air support
c) rocket and missile attacks
d) escorting aircraft.

2 Estimate what fraction of the time is not spent on:

a) air-to-air combat
b) air support
c) rocket and missile attacks
d) escorting aircraft.

3 If the pie chart represents the working hours of the jet over 24 months (2 years), estimate how many months were spent in:

a) air-to-air combat
b) air support
c) rocket and missile attacks
d) escorting aircraft
e) reconnaissance.

Check that your answers add up to a total of 24 months.

WHAT ABOUT THIS?
Over a period of 20 months, a different jet fighter spent one-fifth of its time in air-to-air combat. How many months did it spend in air-to-air combat?

FIGHTER PILOT SELECTION PROCESS

Now you've learned the basics about your aircraft, it's time to choose the other pilots who will make up your squadron.

Becoming a fighter pilot is extremely difficult because there are not many places available and a lot of people apply.

Applicants must be between 17.5 and 25 years old and be between 5 ft 6 in and 6 ft 2 in tall.

Perfect eyesight is essential for fighter pilots.

Fighter pilots must be good problem-solvers and must be confident and calm.

The table below shows nine people who would like to apply for the pilot selection process.

1 How many of the candidates are within the correct age range to become a fighter pilot?

2 Which of the candidates are the correct height to become a fighter pilot?

FIGHTER PILOT CANDIDATES

NAME	M/F	AGE	HEIGHT	EYESIGHT
Luke Sharp	Male	19	5 ft 2 in	perfect
Ben Sherman	Male	16	5 ft 5 in	not perfect
Theo Wood	Male	24	5 ft 9 in	perfect
Emily Connor	Female	25	5 ft 8 in	perfect
Poppy Papadopoulou	Female	28	6 ft 3 in	perfect
Deepa Gorasia	Female	20	5 ft 10 in	not perfect
Simon Davis	Male	36	6 ft 0 in	perfect
Julia Hoffmann	Female	29	6 ft 1 in	perfect
Devon Richardson	Male	22	5 ft 6 in	perfect

WHAT ABOUT THIS?

Find out your own height and see how many more inches you need to grow to be able to apply to be a fighter pilot. How much older do you need to be?

3 Three of the candidates have the correct height, the preferred age, and perfect eyesight. Who are they and are they male or female?

FIGHTER PILOT TRAINING

With your squadron selected, it's time to climb into the cockpit and start your training.

Trainee pilots start by learning about flying regulations, navigation, and the weather. They also learn how aircraft work.

They will learn how to fly on flight simulators and training aircraft, before moving onto jet fighters.

The training is very tiring with 12-hour days. This is to ensure that pilots learn to cope with stressful situations.

1 Write the time (using the words 'o'clock', 'past', or 'to') that a pilot starts:

a) Physical training
b) Emergency procedures test
c) Flight schedule planning
d) Flight grading
e) Daily written exam.

2 Write how many minutes there are from the start of each activity below, to the start of the activity the pilot must do next:

a) Morning briefing
b) Flight schedule planning
c) Flight grading
d) Daily written exam.

A TYPICAL DAY IN PILOT TRAINING

06:00	Studying flight regulations
07:00	Physical training
09:00	Morning briefing
09:30	Emergency procedures test
10:15	Studying weather conditions
10:45	Flight schedule planning
12:00	Meal time
12:30	Simulated flight practice
15:55	Flighl grading
16:40	Daily written exam
18:00	Rest and private study time

3 Write the activity that the pilot is doing at:

a)

b)

c)

d)

e)

f)

WHAT ABOUT THIS?
If a pilot trains for 12 hours each day, six days a week and for eight weeks, how many hours of training is this?

PILOT CALCULATIONS

While on a mission, you will have to make very quick calculations about a wide range of things.

These will include calculating the distance to other aircraft, including your target.

The information from your fighter's displays will also help you to work out how much fuel you have left and whether you need to **ascend** or **descend**.

You can use your fighter's speed to work out how long it will take to reach a target.

ROAR

You are flying at 5.8 miles above the ground, going at a speed of 310 mph.

The controller tells you to descend to 3.4 miles above the ground. You have also been advised to slow down to 220 mph.

1 How many miles must you descend?

2 By how many miles per hour must you slow down?

3 Once you reach 220 mph, you stay at this speed. How long would it take you to travel:

a) 220 mph? b) 110 mph? c) 55 mph?

4 If you are flying at 360 mph, how far would you travel in:

a) one minute?
b) two minutes?
c) three minutes?
d) five minutes?

5 a) How long would a 50-mile journey take flying at 500 mph?
b) How much longer would it take flying at 200 mph?

6 How much longer would a 90-mile journey take flying at 540 mph than at 900 mph?

WHAT ABOUT THIS?
If you know that your jet fighter is traveling at a speed of 12 miles per minute, what must you multiply by to work out the speed in miles per hour?

IN THE COCKPIT

When you're in the cockpit of a jet fighter, you need to be able to read all the dials and information displays.

Jet fighter pilots have to wear special helmets and face masks while flying.

These helmets are attached to cameras all the way around the aircraft—the pilots can even see an image of what's underneath their aircraft!

Some helmets also include night vision technology, so that pilots can "see" targets in the dark.

FORMATION FLYING

When flying with the rest of your squadron, you will have to fly close together in formation (organized patterns).

Here are some simple flying formations.

1 Write how many jets are in formation:

a) 1 b) 2 c) 3 d) 4.

2 Name the shapes made by the jets in formation:

a) 1 b) 2 c) 3 d) 4.

3 **Triangular numbers** are special numbers that can be arranged in a triangle. Each row in the triangle has one more than the row in front of it. Triangular numbers include 3, 6 and 10.

This picture shows six jets in a triangular formation. Row 2 has one more jet than row 1, and row 3 has one more jet than row 2.

a) Write out the first six triangular numbers.
b) Is it possible for 36 jets to fly in a triangular formation?

Row 1 →

Row 2 →

Row 3 →

WHAT ABOUT THIS?
Four jets fly in a square formation with the same number in each row and column. How many more jets are needed to make the next largest square formation?

G-FORCE

When performing aerobatic twists and turns in your jet fighter, you will experience high g-forces (gravitational forces).

G-forces pull on you and can make you feel heavier. You will have the same experience when riding a roller coaster.

WOOOSH!

1-g feels the same as the Earth's normal pull of gravity. 2-g makes you feel twice as heavy, 3-g makes you feel three times as heavy and so on. Pilots train to cope with g-forces inside a large machine called a centrifuge.

Making very sharp turns in a jet fighter can create g-forces of up to 12-g! High g-forces can damage the human body.

G-suits are worn by pilots to help protect them. These suits allow pilots to withstand more extreme maneuvers than they would without the suit.

G-suits are really helpful when making sharp turns or spinning upside-down.

Scientists use units called newtons (N) to measure weight.

1 For a pilot weighing 800 N, write how heavy he would feel at:

a) 2-g b) 3-g c) 4-g d) 5-g e) 6-g f) 7-g
g) 8-g h) 9-g i) 10-g j) 11-g k) 12-g.

2 A fighter pilot experiences 3-g during a maneuver. How heavy would she feel if she normally weighs:

a) 370 N? b) 430 N? c) 570 N? d) 680 N?

3 This picture shows a jet fighter making a turn. How many degrees has the fighter turned through?

WHAT ABOUT THIS?
It is possible to feel a g-force of zero, or 0-g, when you feel weightless. This can happen when a jet is in a dive. Find your own weight and see what you would weigh at 0-g, 1-g, 2-g, 3-g, 4-g and so on.

WEATHER DATA

A jet fighter pilot needs to understand weather conditions. Clouds can cause turbulence and if the wind is blowing strongly, it could blow you off course.

This **line graph** shows the strength and direction of the wind during one day.

RECONNAISSANCE

One of your tasks is to fly over enemy positions, taking photographs. This is known as a reconnaissance mission.

A jet fighter has cameras for taking pictures of the location.

A reconnaissance mission gathers information about a particular place. The aim could be to look for possible targets or find out the enemy's position.

This photo was taken on a reconnaissance mission.

1. Write the co-ordinates for each position:

    a) 1 b) 2 c) 3 d) 4 e) 5 f) 6.

2. In what direction would you fly to go:

    a) from 4 to 1? b) from 2 to 5?
    c) from 3 to 1? d) from 5 to 4?
    e) from 4 to 6? f) from 2 to 6?

This map shows a school, hospital and a civilian area that would not be targets.

3. Count squares and half squares to estimate the area of:

    a) the school
    b) the hospital
    c) the civilian area.

hospital

civilian area

school

WHAT ABOUT THIS?
What fraction of the whole diagram is not covered by the school, hospital or civilian area? Write your fraction in its **simplest form**.

AIR-TO-AIR COMBAT

When flying, your jet fighter can be turned in three different ways. These are known as roll, yaw, and pitch.

If a jet is flying forward in a straight line it can be rolled so one wing is lower than the other one.

Yaw means a turn which, when flying **horizontally**, turns the jet to point to a different compass direction.

Pitch is moving the jet so the front of the jet tilts up or down.

① Describe the series of turns shown in these pictures, saying how many right angles or half-right angle turns are being made each time. Include the words "clockwise" and "counterclockwise" in your descriptions.

A.

B.

C.

② Which of these pictures shows jet fighters flying on **parallel** flight-paths?

A.

B.

C.

D.

E.

WHAT ABOUT THIS?
Which of the jets in question 2 are flying horizontally? Which are flying **vertically**?

29

ANSWERS

Congratulations! Your squadron is ready for action! Check your answers here to see how well you did.

PAGES 4–5

1. a) 60 mph   b) 190 mph   c) 230 mph
   d) 250 mph e) 540 mph f) 800 mph

2. 1,520 mph

3. a) 40 b) 80

4. a) 835 mph   b) 910 mph
   c) 1,445 mph d) 1,140 mph

PAGES 6–7

1. a) Chengdu J-10 b) Chengdu J-10
   c) F-22 Raptor   d) Chengdu J-10

2. Eurofighter Typhoon

3. a) 11.3 ft, b) 1.6 ft, c) 10.7 ft

4. a) 41,000 lb b) 9,300 lb c) 13,500 lb

PAGES 8–9

1. The turbojet was invented.

2. MiG 19

3. 16

4. 64

5. F-22 Raptor

6. 67

PAGES 10–11

1. Approximately: a) ¼ b) ⅓ c) ⅛ d) ¹⁄₁₂

2. Approximately: a) ¾ b) ⅔ c) ⅞ d) ¹¹⁄₁₂

3. a) 6 months b) 8 months c) 3 months
   d) 2 months e) 5 months

WHAT ABOUT THIS? The jet fighter spent
   4 months in air-to-air combat.

PAGES 12–13

1. 5

2. Theo, Emily, Deepa, Simon, Julia, Devon

3. Theo, Emily, Devon (male, female and male)

PAGES 14–15

1. a) seven o'clock
   b) half past nine
   c) quarter to eleven
   d) five to four
   e) twenty to five

2. a) 30 minutes b) 75 minutes c) 45 minutes
   d) 80 minutes

3. a) Physical training
   b) Morning briefing
   c) Studying weather conditions
   d) Simulated flight practice
   e) Flight grading
   f) Daily written exam

WHAT ABOUT THIS? A pilot will spend
   576 hours training.

PAGES 16–17

1. 2.4 miles

2. 90 miles per hour

3. a) 1 hour, b) ½ hour or 30 minutes
   c) ¼ hour or 15 minutes

4. a) 6 miles, b) 12 miles, c) 18 miles,
   d) 30 miles

5. a) 6 minutes b) 9 minutes

6. 4 minutes

WHAT ABOUT THIS? You would need to
   multiply it by 60. 12 x 60 = 720 mph.

PAGES 18–19

1. a) 870 mph b) 0.3-g c) 3 ft/s²
   d) –20 ft/s² e) 0.4 ft f) 480 ft
   g) 700 mph h) 1800 gallons i) 460 gallons
   j) 280 ft/s k) 0.65 ft l) 30 ft/s²

WHAT ABOUT THIS? The tanks have 250
   gallons of fuel left.

PAGES 20–21

1. a) 9 b) 4 c) 5 d) 5

2. a) square b) rhombus c) pentagon
   d) quadrilateral or trapezoid

3. a) 1, 3, 6, 10, 15, 21 b) yes

WHAT ABOUT THIS? Five more jets are
   needed to make the next largest square
   formation (nine in total).

PAGES 22–23

1. a) 1,600 N b) 2,400 N
   c) 3,200 N d) 4,000 N
   e) 4,800 N f) 5,600 N
   g) 6,400 N h) 7,200 N
   i) 8,000 N j) 8,800 N
   k) 9,600 N

2. a) 1,110 N b) 1,290 N
   c) 1,710 N d) 2,040 N

3. 180°

PAGES 24–25

1. a) 10 km/h b) 35 km/h c) 45 km/h
   d) 40 km/h e) 20 km/h f) 40 km/h

2. a) 12:00 and 16:30 b) 12:30 and 16:00 c) 9:30
   and 11:00 d) 10:00, 11:30, and 17:00

3. 08:00 North, 09:00 Northwest, 10:00 North,
   11:00 Northeast, 12:00 Southeast, 13:00 East,
   14:00 East, 15:00 Northeast, 16:00 Northwest,
   17:00 Southwest

4. 15:00

5. 15°

PAGES 26–27

1. a) (2, 6) b) (6, 5) c) (9, 6) d) (2, 3)
   e) (3, 2) f) (8, 3)

2. a) North b) Southwest c) West
   d) Northwest e) East f) Southeast

3. a) 4 squares b) 15½ squares c) 36½ squares

WHAT ABOUT THIS? 112/168 or ⅔

PAGES 28–29

1. a) right angle turn clockwise, half right angle
   turn clockwise, half right angle turn
   clockwise, two right angled turn (clockwise
   or counterclockwise)
   b) half right angle turn counterclockwise,
   half right angle turn counterclockwise, two
   right angled turns (clockwise or
   counterclockwise), right angle turn clockwise
   c) right angle counterclockwise, half right
   angle turn clockwise, right angle turn
   counterclockwise, half right angle turn
   clockwise.

2. a, b, and e pairs are parallel

WHAT ABOUT THIS? The jets in "A" are
   horizontal and the jets in "B" are vertical.

GLOSSARY

ANGLE
An angle is an amount of turn. It is measured in degrees, such as 90°, which is also known as a right angle.

AREA
The area of a shape is the amount of surface it covers.

ASCEND
Ascend means going up.

DESCEND
Descend means going down.

FRACTION
A part of a whole. The number on the bottom (the denominator) tells you how many parts the whole has been split into. The number on the top (the numerator) tells you the number of equal parts being described.

HORIZONTALLY
When something is going from side to side, like the horizon.

LINE GRAPH
A line graph shows information by using points and lines on a grid.

PARALLEL
Parallel lines stay the same distance apart along their entire length. No matter how long the lines are, they would never meet.

SCALES
Scales are usually divided into equal sections and have a marker, such as an arrow, to show values. It is important to work out the value of each section to find the marked value.

SIMPLEST FORM
A fraction can be written in its simplest form by dividing the numerator (top number) and denominator (bottom number) by the largest number possible.

TIMELINE
A timeline is a line that shows events in chronological (date) order.

TRIANGULAR NUMBERS
A triangular number can be drawn as a pattern of dots to make a triangle. Examples include 1, 3, 6, and 10. The sequence follows a +2, +3, +4, +5... pattern.

VERTICALLY
When something goes straight up.

INDEX